Great Peace
for
The Storms of Life

Other Books by Shirley D. Hicks

Great Peace for New Beginnings

Great Peace for Today

Great Peace for Mothers

Great Peace for Women

Great Peace for Men

Great Peace for Ministers

Great Peace for Wives

Great Peace for Leaders

Great Peace for Using Your Gifts & Talents

and others…

A companion journal is available for each
book in the series.

See all of the books and journals in the
Great Peace Series for Christian Living at:

www.GreatPeace.com

Great Peace
for
The Storms of
Life

*How to Find Peace in Difficult Times
from People in the Bible*

SHIRLEY D. HICKS

Great Peace Enterprises LLC
Alexandria, VA

www.GreatPeace.com

Dedicated
to every person who needs
peace in the storms of life

CONTENTS

ACKNOWLEDGEMENTS

I would like to thank my Lord and Savior, Jesus Christ, for giving me this book and the opportunity to share it with people everywhere.

I would also like to thank my husband, Chris, and my daughter, Christen, for their love, support, and help in writing this book.

INTRODUCTION

The storms of life are inevitable. You will surely encounter them at some time in your Christian walk. When you are in the midst of a storm in your life, God does not want you to live in worry and despair. The Bible has promises of peace, encouragement, and direction for you as you face the storms of life. You can find great peace in knowing and applying the Word of God to your situation.

Great Peace for the Storms of Life can help provide the peace you need in facing the difficult times. This book contains ten themes that address some of the most common problems that you may face. Each theme focuses on a particular person in the Bible. It also includes biblical insights, an inspirational poem, and scriptures that incorporate the theme in a powerful way.

You will discover ten people, ten problems, and ten ways in which God can help you in your storm. As you see how God worked in the lives of people in the Bible, you will find great peace in knowing that He can also help you as you face the storms of life.

www.GreatPeace.com

Great peace have they which love thy law:
and nothing shall offend them.
Psalm 119:165

For thou hast been a strength to the poor,
a strength to the needy in his distress,
a refuge from the storm.
Isaiah 25:4

Advance in Adversity

~

Joseph

Joseph

Jacob loved Joseph more than any of his other children because Joseph had been born to him in his old age.
Genesis 37:3 (NLT)

Who was Joseph?

Joseph was one of Jacob's twelve sons and Rachel's eldest son.

Where is his story?

His story is in Genesis 30–50.

What problem did he face?

Joseph was his father's favorite son, which made his ten brothers very jealous of him. When he was seventeen, they sold him as a slave to merchants who took him to Egypt.

How did God work in his life?

Joseph was a young man of integrity and faith. He suffered many hardships when his brothers sold him as a slave, but God blessed his life in an extraordinary way. Over time, he became a great ruler in Egypt, second in command to Pharaoh. His administrative and dream-interpreting skills helped to save Egypt and the surrounding regions from famine.

Adversity and difficult times in life are unavoidable. God, however, can use the adversity that you face to prepare you for the plan and purpose He has for your life. The adversity that Joseph faced is an example of how God uses our difficult circumstances to bless us and make us a blessing to others.

God gave Joseph a dream at a young age that he would someday be a great leader. His brothers, however, were jealous of him and sold him to merchants who took him to Egypt. In Egypt, Joseph faced many harsh circumstances. Yet, God used the adversity to prepare him for a greater purpose. Joseph discovered that he had administrative skills and a gift of interpreting dreams. God used his gifts and blessed him to rise from being a slave to becoming a great ruler in Egypt.

When you face adversity, trust God for the things you cannot control or understand. Sometimes the trials of life can be numerous and hard to bear. Just as in Joseph's life, God has a purpose for everything He allows to come into your life. The adversity can prepare you for a greater work that God has for you to do. If you continue to trust Him in the tough times, you will see that you can advance in adversity as God plans His best for you.

7

Joseph Shows Us…

God will give you a dream for your life.
At a very young age, God began showing Joseph many things about his future. He put a dream in Joseph's heart of achieving greatness. Perhaps the dream gave Joseph hope and inspiration during the times of intense adversity.

Your gifts will open doors for you.
Regardless of where Joseph was, he succeeded because of the gifts that God placed in him. He excelled as a slave and as a prisoner because of his administrative and dream-interpreting skills.

God can work all things together for your good.
Joseph's brothers badly mistreated him, but God caused it all to work together for good for Joseph, his family, and many other people. They did an evil thing to Joseph, but God used what they intended for evil and worked it all together for his good.

You intended to harm me, but God intended it all for good. He brought me to this position so I could save the lives of many people. Genesis 50:20 (NLT)

In Your Life…

What dream has God given you for your life?
Surely, God has placed a dream in your heart.
What is it? Let your God-given dream give
you hope and inspiration during the times of
intense adversity, and trust God to show you
how to bring your dream to fruition.

What gifts has God given you?
Regardless of who you are, God has also
placed gifts and talents inside of you. What
are they? If you are not sure, ask God to show
them to you. Then allow Him to use them so
that you can fulfill the dream that is in your
heart.

Can you see ways in which God is working?
Even when other people badly mistreat you,
God can cause it all to work together for your
good. He can take what they intended for evil
and bring about wonderful blessings for you,
your family, and many other people. Believe
that He knows what is best for you.

**Even in adversity,
God knows best.**

God Knows Best

"For I know the plans I have for you," says the
LORD. "They are plans for good and not for
disaster, to give you a future and a hope."
Jeremiah 29:11 (NLT)

Some things in your life may seem unfair,
And you may feel like God does not care.
Bad things may happen, your plans may fail,
And you pray and pray to no avail.

You may not understand what it all means,
But do not doubt and give up your dreams.
You must remember in all you go through,
God really knows what is best for you.

He never promised that life would be grand,
Without any problems or failed plans,
But He promised always to be by your side,
To be your help, your friend, and your guide.
So, always remember in all you go through,
He is really planning His best for you.

****

Promises for Adversity

But He knoweth the way that I take: when He hath tried me, I shall come forth as gold.

Job 23:10

These trials will show that your faith is genuine. It is being tested as fire tests and purifies gold—though your faith is far more precious than mere gold. So when your faith remains strong through many trials, it will bring you much praise and glory and honor on the day when Jesus Christ is revealed to the whole world.

I Peter 1:7 (NLT)

Behold, I have refined thee, but not with silver; I have chosen thee in the furnace of affliction.

Isaiah 48:10

When you go through deep waters, I will be with you. When you go through rivers of difficulty, you will not drown. When you walk through the fire of oppression, you will not be burned up; the flames will not consume you.

Isaiah 43:2 (NLT)

11

For he hath said, I will never leave thee, nor forsake thee.

Hebrews 13:5

And let us not be weary in well doing: for in due season we shall reap, if we faint not.

Galatians 6:9

Blessed is the man that endureth temptation: for when he is tried, he shall receive the crown of life, which the Lord hath promised to them that love him.

James 1:12

Wherefore seeing we also are compassed about with so great a cloud of witnesses, let us lay aside every weight, and the sin which doth so easily beset us, and let us run with patience the race that is set before us.

Hebrews 12:1

And we know that all things work together for good to them that love God, to them who are the called according to his purpose.

Romans 8:28

He promises peace to his people.

Psalm 85:8 (NIV)

You must remember in all you go through,
God really knows what is best for you.

Defy Discouragement

~

David

David

So Samuel took the horn of oil and anointed him in the presence of his brothers, and from that day on the Spirit of the LORD came powerfully upon David.
1 Samuel 16:13 (NIV)

Who was David?

David was the second king of Israel and one of the ancestors of Jesus Christ.

Where is his story?

His story is in I Samuel 16–1Kings 2.

What problem did he face?

David faced many problems throughout his life that left him discouraged. However, he constantly placed his hope in the Lord.

How did God work in his life?

Through the many trials, difficult situations, and mistakes that David experienced, God ultimately helped him to be victorious in his life. As a shepherd boy, a fugitive, and a great king, David defied discouragement and always put his trust in the Lord. When God chose David to be the king, He referred to David as a man after His own heart.

15

Do you feel as if your situations and circumstances will never change? You may feel as if your prayers are simply bouncing off the ceiling, but they are not. Jesus said in John 11:41-42, "Father, I thank thee that thou hast heard me. And I knew that thou hearest me always." Be encouraged in knowing that God is listening to your prayers.

David was a shepherd boy in Bethlehem who became one of Israel's greatest kings. In the course of his life, David experienced situations that left him discouraged, but he never stopped depending on God. He wrote in Psalm 34:15, "The eyes of the Lord are upon the righteous, and his ears are open unto their cry." David realized that God hears us when we pray, and He is often working in ways we may not see nor understand. As we obey Him, trust Him, and believe that He is going to help us, we can overcome feelings of discouragement.

Regardless of how things may look in your life, you must keep praying and trusting God. He is ready and willing to help you face every storm you encounter. You can climb the mountain, walk through the valley, and win the battle when God is with you. God will help you as you face the storms of life.

David Shows Us…

Problems often accompany blessing.
David experienced tremendous blessings, but new problems often accompanied them. Yet, he decided not to live in discouragement and despair. Instead, David trusted God in the good times and in the difficult times.

God will provide His guidance.
David had times in his life when he simply did not know what to do. In Psalm 32:8, God said to David, "I will instruct thee and teach thee in the way which thou shalt go: I will guide thee with mine eye." In times of discouragement, David prayed and asked God for guidance.

Never stop depending on God.
David became a powerful king, but he realized in the many challenges he encountered that he still needed God to help him. In his triumphs, trials, and tragedies, David discovered that he could not be successful without depending on God in every aspect of his life.

My help comes from the LORD, the Maker of heaven and earth. Psalm 121:1-2 (NIV)

In Your Life...

Do you feel discouraged in difficult times?
God does not want you to live in discouragement. Like David, you must trust God in the good times and in the troubled times. The problems of life are inescapable, but the grace, mercy, and power of God are everlasting.

Have you asked God for guidance?
In the times when you simply do not know what to do, ask God to guide you. He is willing to direct you and show you which way to go and what to do. Jesus said in John 16:13 that His Spirit will guide you into all truth.

Have you asked God for help?
As you face challenging times in your life, remember that you can always look to God for help. In your triumphs, trials, and tragedies, God is able to help you. He never gave up on David and He will never give up on you. He is able and willing to help you. Ask Him to help you today.

**In difficult times,
God will help you.**

God Will Help You

Fear not; I will help thee.
Isaiah 41:13

God has a purpose and God has a plan,
For all you cannot see nor understand.
You must trust Him and allow Him to be,
The God of your life, unconditionally.
His purpose and will, you must keep pursuing,
And believe that He knows what He is doing.
For the times in your life when you feel low,
He will help you to live, to learn, and to grow.

He will help you win the battles you fight,
He will help you endure the darkest of nights.
He will help you to win, to rise, to stand,
He will help you dream and believe you can.
Yes, God has a purpose and God has a plan,
For all you cannot see nor understand.
So trust Him now and allow Him to be,
The God of your life, unconditionally.

****

Promises for Discouragement

For I will turn their mourning into joy, and will comfort them, and make them rejoice from their sorrow.

Jeremiah 31:13

The LORD himself goes before you and will be with you; he will never leave you nor forsake you. Do not be afraid; do not be discouraged.

Deuteronomy 31:8 (NIV)

Then spake Jesus again unto them, saying, I am the light of the world: he that followeth me shall not walk in darkness, but shall have the light of life.

John 8:12

The righteous cry, and the Lord heareth, and delivereth them out of all their troubles.

Psalm 34:17

And God shall wipe away all tears from their eyes.

Revelation 7:17

Why am I discouraged? Why is my heart so sad? I will put my hope in God! I will praise him again— my Savior and my God!

Psalm 42:11 (NLT)

The LORD is good to those who depend on him, to those who search for him.

Lamentations 3:25 (NLT)

But thou, O LORD, art a shield for me; my glory, and the lifter up of mine head.

Psalm 3:3

But ye are a chosen generation, a royal priesthood, an holy nation, a peculiar people; that ye should shew forth the praises of him who hath called you out of darkness into his marvellous light:

1 Peter 2:9

For he has rescued us from the kingdom of darkness and transferred us into the Kingdom of his dear Son, who purchased our freedom and forgave our sins.

Colossians 1:13-14 (NLT)

Blessed are those whose strength is in you.

Psalm 84:5 (NIV)

He will help you win the battles you fight,
And help you endure the darkest nights.

Fight the Fear

~

Hezekiah

Hezekiah

Then King Hezekiah and the prophet Isaiah son of Amoz cried out in prayer to God in heaven.
2 Chronicles 32:20 (NLT)

Who was Hezekiah?
Hezekiah was a king of Judah who loved and feared God.

Where is his story?
His story is in 2 Kings 16:20-20:21, 2 Chronicles 28:27-33, and Isaiah 36:1-3.

What problem did he face?
The Assyrian army had defeated many other kings in the surrounding regions and was planning an attack against Jerusalem. Hezekiah and the people of Judah were afraid.

How did God work in his life?
God assured Hezekiah that He would not allow the Assyrians to harm them. The same night, an angel of the Lord smote the Assyrian army and thousands of the men died. The rest of the army retreated and went home. Hezekiah and his army did not have to fight because God miraculously delivered them.

In II Chronicles 32, Hezekiah, the King of Judah was facing a fearful situation. The King of Assyria was planning an attack against Jerusalem, and he had defeated many other kings in the surrounding regions. In his fear, Hezekiah turned to the Lord in prayer for divine direction and help. Hezekiah encouraged the people by saying, "With us is the Lord our God to help us, and to fight our battles." The same night, God miraculously delivered them from the Assyrian army.

Today, you also have the Lord your God to help you fight your battles. Sometimes situations in your life may be so intense that you become afraid. You may fear what might happen or what might go wrong. Will God send a blessing or give deliverance? David said to the Lord in Psalm 56:3, "What time I am afraid, I will trust in thee." You can be free of fear when you trust in the Lord.

Replace your fears with faith in the Word of God. Believe that God has not given you the spirit of fear, but of power, love, and a sound mind. When you trust Him and walk by faith, He will fight for you, and you will have no reason to be afraid. Give the Lord the situation you are facing, and He will give you the courage to endure the storm.

25

Hezekiah Shows Us…

God knew Hezekiah needed encouragement.
God sent a message of encouragement to Hezekiah and the people of Judah through the prophet, Isaiah, to assuage their fears. He understood that they needed a word of comfort to remind them of His divine protection and help.

God is omnipotent.
Although the King of Assyria was extremely powerful, he was no match for God. The Israelites were able to live in peace because their omnipotent God delivered them from the powerful enemy.

Trust God to do it His way.
God saved Hezekiah and the people of Judah in an unconventional way. They did not have to fight in a battle because God sent an angel to deal with the enemy. Hezekiah trusted God to deliver them in the way He chose to do it.

"He may have a great army, but they are merely men. We have the LORD our God to help us and to fight our battles for us!"
Hezekiah's words greatly encouraged the people.
2 Chronicles 32:8 (NLT)

In Your Life…

Does God understand when you are afraid?
Yes, God understands your fears. As in Hezekiah's life, He will send you a word of comfort when you are afraid to remind you of His divine protection and help.

Do you believe God is omnipotent?
You may be facing an extremely powerful enemy today, but your enemy is no match for God. He has more power than any enemy you will ever have to face. Jesus said in Matthew 28:18, "All power is given to me in Heaven and in earth." Believe that you serve an omnipotent God who can deliver you.

Do you trust God to do it His way?
You may be thinking of a certain way that you expect God to deliver you, but He may send His deliverance in an unconventional way. Do not be afraid. Be open to God's will, and trust Him to deliver you in whatever way He chooses to do so.

**When you are afraid,
trust in the Lord.**

I Will Trust in You

What time I am afraid, I will trust in thee.
Psalm 56:3

The storms of my life are raging,
And the winds are very strong,
My heart is growing fearful,
But I am trying to hold on.
My soul is deeply troubled,
And I do not know what to do.
But every time I am afraid,
Lord, I will trust in you.

I will trust you in my sorrow,
I will trust you in my pain,
In my difficult situation,
In the fierce wind and rain.
I will trust you in this storm,
I know your promises are true,
Yes, every time I am afraid,
Lord, I will trust in you.

****

Promises for Fear

Fear thou not; for I am with thee: be not dismayed; for I am thy God: I will strengthen thee; yea, I will help thee; yea, I will uphold thee with the right hand of my righteousness.

Isaiah 41:10

Say to them that are of a fearful heart, Be strong, fear not: behold, your God will come with vengeance, even God with a recompence; he will come and save you.

Isaiah 35:4

Let not your heart be troubled, neither let it be afraid.

John 14:27

Yea, though I walk through the valley of the shadow of death, I will fear no evil: for thou art with me.

Psalm 23:4

So that we may boldly say, The Lord is my helper, and I will not fear what man shall do unto me.

Hebrews 13:6

For God hath not given us the spirit of fear;
but of power, and of love, and of a sound
mind.

2 Timothy 1:7

The name of the LORD is a strong tower: the
righteous runneth into it, and is safe.

Proverbs 18:10

There is no fear in love. But perfect love
drives out fear, because fear has to do with
punishment. The one who fears is not made
perfect in love.

1 John 4:18 (NIV)

You can go to bed without fear; you will lie
down and sleep soundly.

Proverbs 3:24 (NLT)

God is our refuge and strength, a very present
help in trouble.

Psalm 46:1

The LORD is my light and my salvation—
whom shall I fear? The LORD is the
stronghold of my life— of whom shall I be
afraid?

Psalm 27:1 (NIV)

Every time I am afraid,
Lord, I will trust in you.

Guard against Guilt

~

Mary Magdalene

Mary Magdalene

Some women were there, watching from a distance, including Mary Magdalene, Mary (the mother of James the younger and of Joseph), and Salome. They had been followers of Jesus and had cared for him while he was in Galilee.
Mark 15:40-41 (NLT)

Who was Mary Magdalene?

Mary Magdalene was a woman that Jesus miraculously healed.

Where is her story?

Her story is in Luke 8:2, Mark 15:40-47, John 19:25, John 20:1-18.

What problem did she face?

She was possessed with seven demons.

How did God work in her life?

Jesus healed Mary Magdalene by casting seven demons out of her. Afterwards, she followed Him faithfully and was a helper in His ministry. She was one of the women at the cross when He died, and witnessed his burial. Jesus appeared to her first after his resurrection. She told the others He was alive.

We are all born in sin. However, when Jesus saves us, He forgives all of our sins and we walk in a new life with Him. For some people, the transition from the old life to the new is not always easy because the sins of their past still haunt them. However, when Jesus forgives you, He completely forgives you and expects you to move forward with your new life in Him.

Mary Magdalene was a woman from Galilee whom Jesus healed miraculously when He cast seven demons out of her. Imagine the new life she had after the Lord set her free. She did not struggle with a life of guilt and shame because she was free indeed. Mary Magdalene became a loyal disciple and followed Jesus everywhere He went during His earthly ministry. Afterwards, she was also a faithful follower in the early church. Her life proves that you can be free from your past and go forth to live a life that glorifies God.

Lay aside all feelings of guilt today and believe that the blood of Jesus Christ has covered all of your sins. No matter what happened in your past, He has set you free. Whoever Jesus sets free is free indeed. Believe in your heart that you are free indeed, and go forth and do great things for God.

Mary Magdalene Shows Us...

God's grace is sufficient.
We do not know what kind of life Mary Magdalene had lived in the past, but God's grace was able to save, deliver, and set her free from seven demons. It was powerful enough to break every chain in her life and free her from the strongholds that tried to destroy her.

New beginnings are possible.
Mary Magdalene had a new beginning in her life after Jesus healed her. She began following Him and faithfully supported His ministry. She followed Him to the foot of the cross, to the mouth of the tomb, and beyond.

You can do great things for God.
When Jesus cast the seven demons out of Mary, she did not return to a life of guilt and shame. Mary went forth and did great things in the Kingdom of God. Many still consider her today as one of Jesus' most faithful followers and supporters.

He took his twelve disciples with him, along with some women he had healed and from whom he had cast out evil spirits. Among them were Mary Magdalene, from whom he had cast out seven demons. Luke 8:1-2 (NLT)

In Your Life...

Is God's grace sufficient for you?
In spite of the kind of life you lived in the past, the grace of God is able to save, deliver, and set you free. You can have a new life in Christ Jesus and go forth to do great things in the Kingdom of God.

Will you follow Jesus faithfully?
After Jesus delivers you from a life of sin, will you follow Him faithfully as Mary Magdalene did? Be determined to follow him in the good times, through the difficult times, and for the rest of your life.

Are you free indeed?
Satan will try to make you think that you cannot live a life for Jesus, but the power of God makes you free. Isaiah 54:17 reminds us that, "No weapon that is formed against thee shall prosper; and every tongue that shall rise against thee in judgment thou shalt condemn." You are free in Jesus!

**In your new life in Christ,
you must be free.**

36

You Must Be Free

If the Son therefore shall make you free,
ye shall be free indeed.
John 8:36

God is saying to you:

"You are my child and I love you so much,
And I am glad your life has been touched,
By My divine power and My divine grace,
Yet, I see some unrest as I look in your face.

You seem to be troubled; you do not rest,
Though I've given you my Spirit and my best.
Others see your smiles, but when they depart,
I see the guilt that is still in your heart.

The things in your past that you cannot let go,
Your friends cannot see it, but I surely know,
That you are still troubled and hurting inside,
Although in Me, you fully abide.

When I look at you, I say, how could that be,
When I died on a cross just to set you free?

37

When I suffered such hurt and endured pain,
Was all of my suffering for you in vain?

The sins of your past are all forgiven,
But in your past, you are still living,
With so much guilt, with so many sighs,
All constantly nourished by Satan's lies.

The peace of God and a clean heart too,
Are some of the things I died to give you.
So you must not live in guilt today,
Put all of your thoughts of guilt away.

Let go of your guilt and be free at last,
Rest in my love and let go of your past.
And find in my grace all that you need,
Because whom I set free must be free indeed.

You are my child, whom I love very much,
So never forget that your life is touched,
By my divine grace, which always exceeds,
Any sins in your past, so be free indeed!

****

Promises for Guilt

For by grace are ye saved through faith; and that not of yourselves: it is the gift of God.

Ephesians 2:8

But this one thing I do, forgetting those things which are behind, and reaching forth unto those things which are before, I press toward the mark for the prize of the high calling of God in Christ Jesus.

Philippians 3:13-14

And ye shall know the truth, and the truth shall make you free.

John 8:32

But by the grace of God I am what I am: and his grace which was bestowed on me was not in vain.

I Corinthians 15:10

As far as the east is from the west, so far hath he removed our transgressions from us.

Psalm 103:12

And since we have a great High Priest who rules over God's house, let us go right into the presence of God with sincere hearts fully trusting him. For our guilty consciences have been sprinkled with Christ's blood to make us clean, and our bodies have been washed with pure water.

Hebrews 10:21-22 (NLT)

There is therefore now no condemnation to them which are in Christ Jesus, who walk not after the flesh, but after the Spirit. For the law of the Spirit of life in Christ Jesus hath made me free from the law of sin and death.

Romans 8:1-2

I, even I, am he who blots out your transgressions, for my own sake, and remembers your sins no more.

Isaiah 43:25 (NIV)

Verily, verily, I say unto you, He that heareth my word, and believeth on him that sent me, hath everlasting life, and shall not come into condemnation; but is passed from death unto life.

John 5:24

Let go of your guilt and be free at last,
Rest in my love and let go of your past.

Nurture the Need

~

The Shunammite Woman

The Shunammite Woman

At the end of the seven years she came back from the land of the Philistines and went to appeal to the king for her house and land.
2 Kings 8:3 (NIV)

Who was the Shunammite Woman?
The Shunammite woman was a wealthy woman who gave generously to the prophet Elisha when he traveled through her land. Elisha also raised her son from the dead.

Where is her story?
Her story is in II Kings 8.

What problem did she face?
She wanted the king to restore her property.

How did God work in her life?
Elisha advised the Shunammite woman to move away to another land because of an impending famine. When she later returned, she went to the king to request the property she had left behind. The king was already talking to Elisha's servant about her when she arrived. He immediately restored all of her income and property back to her.

43

God knows about all of your needs and He is able and willing to take care of you. The life of the Shunammite woman in II Kings 8 demonstrates this truth. This woman had been very hospitable to the prophet Elisha as he traveled through her land. She and her husband built a special room for Elisha and provided meals for him during his stays. One day, Elisha advised them to move away to another land because of an imminent famine.

She returned to her homeland after the famine was over and went to the king to request the property she left behind. When she arrived, it was no coincident that Elisha's servant, Gehazi, was telling the king about how Elisha had raised her son from the dead. The king immediately restored all of her property to her. God provided for her in the famine and upon her return to her homeland.

In similar ways, God will supply your needs when you walk according to His Word and use wisely the resources He gives you. He does not want you to worry about the problems that you face, but to trust Him in everything. Regardless of what your needs are, Ephesians 3:20 says, God "is able to do exceeding abundantly above all that we ask or think." He will provide all that you need.

The Shunammite Woman Shows Us...

Honor the Lord and trust Him to take care of you.
The Shunammite woman and her husband blessed the prophet, Elisha. God, in return, blessed them not only with a son, but also in settling a great legal matter.

The Lord will go before you to prepare a way.
Even in a legal situation, the Lord went before the Shunammite woman to prepare a way for her victory. He orchestrated the circumstance so that she stood before the king and Gehazi just as they were speaking of her.

God will touch the hearts of other people to bless you.
God touched the heart of the king to work on the Shunammite woman's behalf. After he verified her story, the king immediately assigned an official to her case to restore all of the income and property she had left behind.

The king asked the woman about it, and she told him. Then he assigned an official to her case and said to him, "Give back everything that belonged to her, including all the income from her land from the day she left the country until now."
2 Kings 8:6 (NIV)

In Your Life...

Are you honoring the Lord?
As Christians, we fund the work of the Kingdom of God when we give our tithes and offerings. God wants you to give to His work as He blesses you. He promised to bless you when you are a blessing to His Kingdom and to others.

Is God going before you to prepare a way?
Philippians 4:19 says, "But my God shall supply all your need." Whether your need is legal, physical, financial, emotional, or of some other type, God can go before you and prepare the way to supply it.

Whose heart is God touching to bless you?
Only God could have touched the king's heart to bless the Shunammite woman in such a tremendous way. God can also touch someone's heart in your life and arrange things in your favor so that you will have everything you need, just when you need it.

**God will give you
all that you need.**

All I Need

For your Father knows what you need
before you ask him.
Matthew 6:8 (NIV)

I find in Jesus all that I need,
To help me live and succeed,
In all the trials and tests I face,
With every problem, in every place.
Sometimes, all my desires, indeed,
Outweigh the things I really need,
But He is so kind and lovingly,
Gives whatever is best for me.

God's schedule is often not like mine,
But in His way and in His time,
He opens doors and makes a way,
And leads me to a brighter day.
I do not fear and I do not fret,
Because He's never failed me yet,
But He supplies all I need,
When I trust Him and believe.

****

Promises for Need

If ye then, being evil, know how to give good gifts unto your children, how much more shall your Father which is in heaven give good things to them that ask him?

Matthew 7:11

Let us therefore come boldly unto the throne of grace, that we may obtain mercy, and find grace to help in time of need.

Hebrews 4:16

Honor the LORD with your wealth and with the best part of everything you produce. Then he will fill your barns with grain, and your vats will overflow with good wine.

Proverbs 3:9-10 (NLT)

Blessed be the Lord, who daily loadeth us with benefits, even the God of our salvation.

Psalm 68:19

For the needy shall not always be forgotten: the expectation of the poor shall not perish for ever.

Psalm 9:18

I was young and now I am old, yet I have never seen the righteous forsaken or their children begging bread.

Psalm 37:25 (NIV)

Jesus replied, "I am the bread of life. Whoever comes to me will never be hungry again. Whoever believes in me will never be thirsty.

John 6:35 (NLT)

O fear the LORD, ye his saints: for there is no want to them that fear him. The young lions do lack, and suffer hunger: but they that seek the LORD shall not want any good thing.

Psalm 34:9

And he said unto his disciples, Therefore I say unto you, Take no thought for your life, what ye shall eat; neither for the body, what ye shall put on. The life is more than meat, and the body is more than raiment.

Luke 12:22-23

LORD, you alone are my inheritance, my cup of blessing. You guard all that is mine.

Psalm 16:5 (NLT)

He opens doors and makes a way,
He leads me to a brighter day.

Shun the Shame

~

The Prodigal Son

The Prodigal Son

I will arise and go to my father, and will say unto
him, Father, I have sinned against heaven,
and before thee.
Luke 15:18

Who was the Prodigal Son?
The prodigal son was a young man in a parable Jesus told to his disciples to demonstrate God's love for His children.

Where is his story?
His story is in Luke 15:11-22.

What problem did he face?
He asked his father for his inheritance, then left home and spent it all in riotous living. When he had nothing left, he returned home, not knowing if his father would accept him.

How did God work in his life?
Using this parable, Jesus showed His disciples that God loves us unconditionally. The son wasted his inheritance in living a rebellious lifestyle and felt ashamed to go back to his father. The father, however, gladly and lovingly received him when he returned home.

Everyone will experience some form of shame in life. When you encounter such situations, you should not concentrate on what other people say or think, but look to Jesus for the strength that you need to endure each situation. If you fall into self-pity, bitterness, and resentment, the situation may overwhelm you. Jesus wants you to trust Him to take you through the most humiliating times of life.

Jesus understands disgrace and shame. His death on the cross was a very humiliating event. Yet, Hebrews 12:2 tells us that it was not in vain. For the joy that was set before Him, Jesus endured the cross, despising the shame, and now He is sitting at the right hand of the throne of God. God used the humiliating event to bring Him glory.

God can also use your shameful situations. No matter what you face, believe in your heart that God is for you. He loves you unconditionally and He can help you endure whatever disgraceful situation you may be facing. Romans 8:31 says, "If God be for us, who can be against us?" Since you have the almighty God on your side, you must believe that something wonderful can come out of your shame because you are a child of God.

The Prodigal Son Shows Us...

Ungodly decisions can be costly.
He discovered that short-term decisions can have long-term consequences. He rushed into a decision that he had to live with for the rest of his life. Although his father received him back home again, his inheritance was gone.

We must come to ourselves.
The prodigal son was living a rebellious life, but he finally came to a place where he knew he should return to his father. He realized that a life of sin was devastating, but a life with his father was full of love and blessings.

His father loved him unconditionally.
His father showed him that he loved him dearly. The son did not have to live in shame because his father was waiting with loving arms to receive him home again. The father's love covered any feelings of shame that the son had, and reminded the son that he was very special to his father.

So he got up and went to his father. "But while he was still a long way off, his father saw him and was filled with compassion for him; he ran to his son, threw his arms around him and kissed him. Luke 15:20 (NIV)

In Your Life…

Are you praying before making any major decisions?
Do not rush into any major decisions before getting God's advice about the situation. Ungodly decisions, especially, can have long-term consequences that you will have to live with for the rest of your life.

Where are you in your life today?
Are you in a place where you know that you should return to your father? Romans 6:23 says, "The wages of sin is death; but the gift of God is eternal life through Jesus Christ our Lord." Repent of any sin in your life and return to the Father.

Can you feel God's love?
Regardless of where you are now, God still loves you dearly. You do not have to live in shame because your Father is waiting with loving, opened arms to receive you again to Himself. His love will cover your feelings of shame and remind you that you are His precious child.

**God's love will
cover your shame.**

My Shame

Casting all your care upon him; for he careth for you.
I Peter 5:7

Lord Jesus,

Look at me and my life today,
I never thought it would be this way.
My head hangs low and I feel so sad,
It is the worse feeling I have ever had.

People are watching, I see the stares,
There is no hiding for me anywhere.
I must face the facts, but who can I blame,
For my feelings of disgrace and shame?

I cannot change the past or make amends,
This is so real and I cannot pretend,
But I know that I am not alone,
I can come boldly to your throne.

Grace is there and mercy too,
Yes, Lord, I can come to you.
Because in your word you have said,

You are the lifter of my head.

With open arms, you welcome me,
And promise me true victory.
My situation, yes, it is real,
But there is no reason I must feel,
Full of shame and despair.
I know that you are always there,

To pick me up each time I fall,
To answer me each time I call,
To help me through every day,
Despite what others do or say.

I must never feel ashamed,
I am your child and I bear your name.
Although I've made some mistakes,
Your love for me is very great.

You love me unconditionally,
It is in these times I really see,
Your love for me is always the same,
And I have no reason to be ashamed.

****

Promises for Shame

Let my heart be sound in thy statues; that I be not ashamed.

Psalm 119:80

The Lord upholdeth all that fall, and raiseth up all those that be bowed down.

Psalm 145:14

This I know; for God is for me.

Psalm 56:9

And ye shall eat in plenty, and be satisfied, and praise the name of the Lord your God, that hath dealt wondrously with you: and my people shall never be ashamed.

Joel 2:26

Looking unto Jesus the author and finisher of our faith; who for the joy that was set before him endured the cross, despising the shame, and is set down at the right hand of the throne of God.

Hebrews 12:2

Blessed is he whose transgression is forgiven, whose sin is covered.

Psalm 32:1

As far as the east is from the west, so far hath he removed our transgressions from us. Like as a father pitieth his children, so the LORD pitieth them that fear him.

Psalm 103:12-13

That is why I am suffering here in prison. But I am not ashamed of it, for I know the one in whom I trust, and I am sure that he is able to guard what I have entrusted to him until the day of his return.

2 Timothy 1:12 (NLT)

If our hearts condemn us, we know that God is greater than our hearts, and he knows everything.

1 John 3:20 (NIV)

Being confident of this, that he who began a good work in you will carry it on to completion until the day of Christ Jesus.

Philippians 1:6 (NIV)

I must never feel ashamed,
I am your child and I bear your name.

Surrender the Sickness

~

The Israelites

The Israelites

*They went out into the wilderness of Shur;
and they went three days in the wilderness,
and found no water.
Exodus 15:22*

Who were the Israelites?

The Israelites were the descendants of Abraham, Isaac, and Jacob.

Where is this story?

This story is in Exodus 15:22-27.

What problem did they face?

God miraculously delivered them from the Egyptians army by parting the Red Sea so they could escape the imminent captivity. Three days later, they could not find any water as they traveled in the dry, hot wilderness.

How did God work in their lives?

When the Israelites finally found water in the wilderness, it was bitter. The Lord told Moses to throw a tree into the waters, and then the bitter waters became sweet. God assured the Israelites that He was the Lord who would always take care of them.

In Exodus 15, Moses was leading the children of Israel through the wilderness of Shur. Three days earlier, they miraculously crossed the Red Sea while the entire Egyptians army drowned in it. That miracle strengthened their faith in both Moses and the Lord. However, as they continued on their journey, they could not find any water. After three days without water, they finally found water in Mara, but it was bitter.

They quickly forgot about the previous victories that the Lord gave them and began to complain. Nevertheless, the Lord showed Moses a tree to cast into the waters that made the bitter waters sweet. Although they had seen God work in the past, He wanted to show them that He was the Lord who could also heal them, or take care of them in any type of desperate situation.

When you face times of sickness, remember that God can help you through the bitterness of life. Surrender your sickness to Him. Then, recall the "Red Sea" experiences He has led you through in the past, and ask Him to show you the solution to your problem. His answer may not be what you expect, but it will be God's best for you. He is the God who will always take care of you.

The Israelites Show Us...

We must remember past victories.
God had performed many great miracles for the Israelites before they reached the wilderness. Yet, they still felt desperate when they could not find water in the wilderness. They focused on their problems instead of God's past provisions.

God can make a way out of no way.
God led them to the exact place where they could find water in the midst of the very dry land. He made a way for them where there seemed to be no way, and showed them that He could make the impossible possible.

There is an answer for the problem.
The answer to their problem was in God's hands. He showed Moses how to heal the water so the people could drink it. God wanted the Israelites to trust and depend on Him in the midst of a desperate situation.

He said, "If you will listen carefully to the voice of the LORD your God and do what is right in his sight, obeying his commands and keeping all his decrees, then I will not make you suffer any of the diseases I sent on the Egyptians; for I am the LORD who heals you." Exodus 15:26 (NLT)

In Your Life…

Has God done anything great for you in the past?
Surely, God has done something great for you
in the past. Think about your past victories
instead of your problems to help you
eliminate any feelings of desperation and
hopelessness.

Does your situation seem impossible?
Jesus said in Luke 18:27, "The things which
are impossible with men are possible with
God." Surrender your impossible situation to
Him. He can lead you to the exact place
where you can find what you need in the
midst of a seemingly impossible situation.

Is there an answer to your problem?
God is omnipotent, omniscience, and
omnipresent. He said in Jeremiah 32:27,
"Behold, I am the LORD, the God of all
flesh: is there any thing too hard for me?" He
can show you what to do in your situation.
Look to Him for the answer. Surrender your
sickness to God, and believe that He is a God
who can heal you.

The Lord can heal you.

The Lord Who Heals You

For I am the Lord that healeth thee.
Exodus 15:26

As thoughts of your sickness are in your head,
Remember God's promises and what He said.

Despite what you feel or what you have heard,
Never forget His promises or His Word.

For God's Word is life and healing too,
He's a faithful God and His promises are true.

God loves you dearly and He really does care,
He will not allow more than you can bear.

Your battle may seem difficult and hard,
But the battle really belongs to the Lord.

He will fight those who fight against you,
Stand still and watch Him take you through.

For your situation is in His control,
One day you will come forth as pure gold.

66

Trust in His word and do not doubt,
In His own time, He will bring you out.

You must not worry, complain, or fret,
Because He is a God who never forgets.

He sees your tears and knows your pain,
But life is full of sunshine and rain.

In every season, He will be your guide,
He will be faithfully by your side,

And stand with you in good times and bad,
When you are happy and when you are sad.

Yes, God is with you, no matter the test,
So always trust Him to do what is best.

Hold to His promises in all you go through,
Because He is the Lord who can heal you.

****

Promises for Sickness

Bless the Lord, O my soul, and forget not all his benefits: who forgiveth all thine iniquities; who healeth all thy diseases.

Psalm 103:2-3

He sent His word, and healed them, and delivered them from their destructions.

Psalm 107:20

Heal me, O Lord, and I shall be healed; save me, and I shall be saved.

Jeremiah 17:14

But he was wounded for our transgressions, he was bruised for our iniquities: the chastisement of our peace was upon him; and with his stripes we are healed.

Isaiah 53:5

For I will restore health unto thee, and I will heal thee of thy wounds, saith the Lord.

Jeremiah 30:17

With his stripes we are healed.

Isaiah 53:5

68

Do not be wise in your own eyes; fear the LORD and shun evil. This will bring health to your body and nourishment to your bones.

Proverbs 3:7-8 (NIV)

You will show me the way of life, granting me the joy of your presence and the pleasures of living with you forever.

Psalm 16:11 (NLT)

My child, pay attention to what I say. Listen carefully to my words. Don't lose sight of them. Let them penetrate deep into your heart, for they bring life to those who find them, and healing to their whole body.

Proverbs 4:20-22 (NLT)

Is any sick among you? let him call for the elders of the church; and let them pray over him, anointing him with oil in the name of the Lord: And the prayer of faith shall save the sick, and the Lord shall raise him up.

James 5:14-15

A large crowd followed him, and he healed all who were ill.

Matthew 12:15 (NIV)

Your battle may seem difficult and hard,
But the battle really belongs to the Lord.

Surpass the Sorrow

~

The Disciples

The Disciples

But because I have said these things unto you,
sorrow hath filled your heart.
John 16:6

Who were the disciples?
The disciples were the twelve men who followed Jesus during His earthly ministry.

Where is their story?
Their story is in John 16:1-22.

What problem did they face?
The disciples were very sad when Jesus told them He was going away. They did not fully understand what He was saying to them, and they had many questions.

How did God work in their lives?
Jesus told His disciples that He would be going away soon, but He comforted them with the promise of His resurrection and ascension. He assured them that their feelings of sorrow would not be permanent. Because of His resurrection power, Jesus told them they would soon see Him again, and then their sorrow would turn into great joy.

As Christians, we know that death is only the beginning of an eternal life with Jesus Christ. However, even for Christians, the loss of a loved one can be difficult. In John 16, the disciples were very sad when Jesus told them He was going away. Jesus said to them, "And ye shall be sorrowful, but your sorrow shall be turned into joy." Jesus knew His death would only be the beginning of something wonderful and everlasting.

When sadness fills your heart because of the loss of a loved one, focus on Jesus' words to His disciples. Paul also reminded us that we are not as those who have no hope. Those who die in Christ are in the presence of God, and one day we will be with them again around God's throne. Yes, one day our sorrow will turn into joy. John wrote in Revelation 21:4, "And God shall wipe away all tears from their eyes; and there shall be no more death, neither sorrow, nor crying, neither shall there be any more pain: for the former things are passed away." In Heaven, we will have no more death, pain, or sorrow. In the midst of your sorrow, remember that you will soon be together again with your loved ones around God' throne. Let this truth surpass any sorrow that lingers in your heart.

73

The Disciples Show Us...

Death brings sorrow.
Although Jesus tried to encourage the disciples, they were still sad because He was going to leave them. Everyone must leave this earth one day, but Paul said in 2 Corinthians 5:8, "We are confident, I say, and willing rather to be absent from the body, and to be present with the Lord." Even in death, we will be with the Lord.

Jesus gives eternal life.
Jesus conquered death and the grave. He said to Martha in John 11:25 (NLT), "I am the resurrection and the life. Anyone who believes in me will live, even after dying." Jesus was telling her that He gives eternal life.

Heaven will be wonderful.
John reminds us that in Heaven, "God shall wipe all tears from their eyes; and there shall be no more death, neither sorrow, nor crying, neither shall there be any more pain." Heaven will be a very wonderful place.

And ye now therefore have sorrow: but I will see you again, and your heart shall rejoice, and your joy no man taketh from you. John 16:22

In Your Life…

Do you have eternal life?

This life is only temporal, and each of us must leave this earth one day. Nevertheless, as Christians, when we are "absent from the body, we are present with the Lord." If you have accepted Jesus as your Lord and Savior, one day you will forever be with the Lord.

Is your hope in Christ?

Because Jesus is the resurrection and the life, your great hope is in knowing that anyone who believes in Him will live, even after dying. When you have eternal life in Jesus Christ, the sorrow that you experience now will become great joy in eternity.

Can you imagine Heaven?

You can find peace in knowing that one day you will be in Heaven with the Lord forever. It is a place where we will have no more death, sorrow, crying, nor pain. Can you imagine that? It will be wonderful!

**One day we will be together
around God's throne.**

Around His Throne

But your sorrow shall be turned into joy.
John 16:20

One day, perhaps quite unexpected,
Yet, still within God's love, protected,
A loved one left this earthly home,
And gathered around the Father's throne.
Although it is painful, you must know,
That God allowed it all to be so.
He knows your feelings and your cares,
And it is not more than you can bear.

Some things you may never understand,
But trust in God's big and glorious plan.
And only let thoughts fill your mind,
Of all your joyful family times.
Do not be sorrowful, but realize,
God will wipe all tears from your eyes,
And rest assured, it will not be long,
Before you are together around God's throne.

****

Promises for Sorrow

And ye now therefore have sorrow: but I will see you again, and your heart shall rejoice, and your joy no man taketh from you.

John 16:22

And God shall wipe all tears from their eyes; and there shall be no more death, neither sorrow, nor crying, neither shall there be any more pain.

Revelation 21:4

Yea, though I walk through the valley of the shadow of death, I will fear no evil: for thou art with me.

Psalm 23:4

We are confident, I say, and willing rather to be absent from the body, and to be present with the Lord.

II Corinthians 5:8

Precious in the sight of the Lord is the death of his saints.

Psalm 116:15

To appoint unto them that mourn in Zion, to give unto them beauty for ashes, the oil of joy for mourning, the garment of praise for the spirit of heaviness; that they might be called trees of righteousness, the planting of the LORD, that he might be glorified.

Isaiah 61:3

Now may our Lord Jesus Christ himself and God our Father, who loved us and by his grace gave us eternal comfort and a wonderful hope, comfort you and strengthen you in every good thing you do and say.

2 Thessalonians 2:16-17 (NLT)

And the ransomed of the LORD shall return, and come to Zion with songs and everlasting joy upon their heads: they shall obtain joy and gladness, and sorrow and sighing shall flee away.

Isaiah 35: 10

You have turned my mourning into joyful dancing. You have taken away my clothes of mourning and clothed me with joy.

Psalm 30:11 (NLT)

You must not grow weary, but realize,
God will wipe all tears from your eyes.

Triumph in Trouble

~

Job

Job

There once was a man named Job who lived in the land of Uz. He was blameless—a man of complete integrity. He feared God and stayed away from evil.
Job 1:1 (NLT)

Who was Job?
Job was a very devout man who was wealthy and generous.

Where is his story?
His story is in the Book of Job.

What problem did he face?
Job faced extreme suffering and great losses.

How did God work in his life?
Although Job lived a very devout life, he also endured much pain and suffering. God allowed Job to experience extreme trials and showed that suffering is not always a form of chastisement. In patience, Job held to his integrity and did not doubt the faithfulness of God, but he questioned the purpose for his suffering. In the end, God doubly blessed his life and he became a role model for having patience in the midst of great trials.

You may anticipate some of the storms that occur in your life, but others may come unexpectedly and leave you stunned, broken, and bruised. Things may happen that you never saw coming. This was the case in Job's life. He lived a very pious life, and was very wealthy and generous. Job 1:1 (NLT) says he was "a man of complete integrity. He feared God and stayed away from evil."

Despite Job's perfect life, one day, quite unexpectedly, he experienced intense trials and heartaches. He lost his ten children, his wealth, and most of his health. Yet, in the midst of his extreme suffering, his faith, patience, and integrity never wavered. The Bible reveals that Satan asked God for permission to test Job's faith, indicating that God was always in control of Job's circumstances. In the end, God blessed Job with twice as much as he had before the trials because of his patience and endurance.

What storm are you facing today? Like Job, trust in the love and faithfulness of God. You may not know about everything that is happening in the spiritual world concerning your life, but you do know that God is in control. Believe that He will take you through the storm and give you double in the end.

Job Shows Us...

Trouble may be unexpected and intense.
Perhaps it was just an ordinary day when the worse imaginable situations began to happen in Job's life. You may never know what your future holds, but you must trust the God who holds your future.

Friends and relatives may not be the best comforters.
Job's wife and three friends did not give him the best advice in his troubles. He did not "curse God and die' as his wife suggested, nor confess the sins he never committed as his three friends recommended. Instead, he said, "I know that my Redeemer lives" and looked to God for deliverance.

God is a refuge in times of trouble.
Although Job had many questions about what was happening in his life, he did not give up on God in the midst of his troubles. When faced with the storms of life, he ran to God, not away from Him.

What? Shall we receive good at the hand of God,
and shall we not receive evil? Job 2:10

In Your Life…

What is happening behind the scenes?
Job's life gives you a behind-the-scenes view of your spiritual warfare. It shows that you have an enemy who seeks to kill, steal, and destroy every good thing God has given you. It also shows that Satan can only do what God allows him to do. God is always in control.

Who is in your inner circle?
Sometimes the people closest to you may not be your best comforters in difficult times. However, you can find the strength, hope, and encouragement you need in times of trouble in the promises in the Word of God.

Can you trust God in your time of trouble?
Like Job, you may also have many questions about what is happening in your life. Nevertheless, hold to God's unchanging hand. Look to Jesus and let Him be a place of strength and comfort for you during the storms of life. He can be a refuge for you.

**Let God be your refuge
from the storms of life.**

A Refuge from the Storm

Oh that I had wings like a dove... I would hasten my
escape from the windy storm and tempest
Psalm 55:6-8

I have come out of the storm, but into rain,
Only to see another storm again.
I was looking for the sun to appear today,
But the sun has gone another way.
The clouds are dark and hanging low,
There is no place where I can go,
Until this tempest passes by,
Until the sunshine lights the sky.

I need a shelter from this storm,
For my heart is weary and worn,
I need a refuge, a hiding place,
Filled with love, compassion, and grace,
To keep me from the boisterous wind,
Until the storm finally ends.

Where can I go, who can I call,
Before the next raindrop falls,
Before flood waters sweep over my soul,

Before I feel the storm's fierce cold?
But what is this that I now hear?
A voice so strong, yet soft and clear.
I see a hand extend to me,
Is this my hope and security?
Now I can see as I look very hard,
This is indeed the hand of God!
And oh, listen, He speaks to me,
He is saying something about victory!

He is saying, "Be of good cheer, it is I,
I will be the sunshine in your sky,
I will be your refuge from this storm,
I will save you with my outstretched arm.

This tempest will no longer toss you about,
With lovingkindness, I will draw you out,
And put you in my secret place,
Where you will find peace, hope, and grace.
So come unto Me, into My arms,
For I am your refuge from this storm!"

****

Promises for Trouble

For thou hast been a strength to the poor, a strength to the needy in his distress, a refuge from the storm.

Isaiah 25:4

The Lord also will be a refuge for the oppressed, a refuge in times of trouble.

Psalm 9:9

Though I walk in the midst of trouble, thou wilt revive me: thou shalt stretch forth thine hand against the wrath of mine enemies, and thy right hand shall save me.

Psalm 138:7

He shall call upon me, and I will answer him: I will be with him in trouble; I will deliver him, and honour him.

Psalm 91:15

The Lord is good, a stronghold in the day of trouble; and He knoweth them that trust in Him.

Nahum 1:7

Thou art my hiding place; thou shalt preserve me from trouble; thou shalt compass me about with songs of deliverance.

Psalm 32:7

The steps of a good man are ordered by the LORD: and he delighteth in his way. Though he fall, he shall not be utterly cast down: for the LORD upholdeth him with his hand.

Psalm 37:23-24

God blesses those who patiently endure testing and temptation. Afterward they will receive the crown of life that God has promised to those who love him.

James 1:12 (NLT)

I will say of the Lord, he is my refuge and my fortress: my God; in him will I trust.

Psalm 91:2

There hath no temptation taken you but such as is common to man: but God is faithful, who will not suffer you to be tempted above that ye are able; but will with the temptation also make a way to escape, that ye may be able to bear it.

1 Corinthians 10:13

I will be your refuge from this storm,
I will save you with my outstretched arm.

Win over Worry

~

Zacharias

Zacharias

But the angel said unto him, Fear not, Zacharias: for thy prayer is heard; and thy wife Elisabeth shall bear thee a son, and thou shalt call his name John.
Luke 1:13

Who was Zacharias?
Zacharias was a priest, husband to Elizabeth, and father of John the Baptist.

Where is his story?
His story is in Luke 1:5-25.

What problem did he face?
He and his wife did not have any children.

How did God work in his life?
An angel appeared to Zacharias and told him he would soon have a son. He and his wife were very old, so Zacharias did not believe it. The angel told Zacharias that he would not be able to speak until after the child was born because of his unbelief. The baby was born just as the angel said and Zacharias named him John. John became a great preacher and was the forerunner for the Messiah.

91

Before the birth of John the Baptist, the angel, Gabriel, appeared unto his father, Zacharias, to tell him he would soon have a son. It seemed so impossible to Zacharias. How could it be? He and his wife were both very old. Zacharias could not believe it. The angel told him that he would not be able to speak until after the child was born because he did not believe it. Zacharias's disbelief did not stop God from fulfilling His plan. The baby was born just as the angel said.

Do you hear God telling you something today that seems impossible? As you listen to His voice, what is your response? Do you really believe He is able to do whatever He is speaking to your heart? God wants you to respond in faith when He tells you that He is going to do something great for you. Walk in faith and believe God when He sends good news to you. No matter how impossible the situation may seem, as the angel told Zacharias in Luke 1:37, "With God nothing shall be impossible." As you face the storms of life, you do not have to worry about things. Your impossible situations are very important to God and He wants to bless you. Listen for His voice today and do not worry, but believe what He speaks to your heart.

Zacharias Shows Us...

God may surprise you with His blessings.
Because he and his wife were both elderly, Zacharias probably thought it was too late for them to have a child. Just imagine how surprised he must have been to know that God was finally answering his prayers.

You must Believe God.
Zacharias did not believe the angel's message. It seemed impossible after so many years of hoping. God, however, can do amazing things. He presented Zacharias with a blessing that was so incredible that he could not believe it even after an angel told him.

God is listening to your prayers.
Zacharias had prayed many years for a child. The angel said to him in Luke 1:13 (NLT), "Don't be afraid, Zacharias! God has heard your prayer. Your wife, Elizabeth, will give you a son, and you are to name him John." God had a divine purpose, plan, and His own timing for answering Zacharias's prayers.

Everyone who heard about it reflected on these events and asked, "What will this child turn out to be?" For the hand of the Lord was surely upon him in a special way. Luke 1:66

In Your Life…

Is it really too late?
You may think that it is too late or you are too old to realize the dream in your heart. Nevertheless, who gave you the dream? God may surprise you with the answer to your long-awaited prayer.

Do you believe what God is saying to you?
Perhaps you have prayed for something for many years. Is God now saying it is going to happen? Can you believe it? Could this storm be ending? If He presents you with a blessing that seems incredible, believe it. With God, all things are possible.

Is your problem important to God?
Everything about you is very important to God, even your seemingly impossible situations. He knows the deepest desire in your heart. He sees your tears, and He knows about all of your worries. God has a divine purpose, plan, and timing for the answer. Do not worry about what you are going through. Trust in His divine will for your life.

You are very important to God.

You Are Very Important to Me

*But many who are the greatest now will be least
important then, and those who seem least important
now will be the greatest then.*
Matthew 19:30 (NLT)

God is saying to you:

"I see you quietly sitting there,
Thinking that I do not care.

I know your heart is weary and worn,
And all your hope is nearly gone.

Your day looks dark and your night is long,
You do not have strength to sing my songs.

I want you to know, I want you to see,
That you are very important to Me.

I may seem far, but I am near,
I know your thoughts and I see your tears.

All of your prayers, I've heard them too,

I have not forsaken or forgotten you.
You are important to Me, the things you do,
And the problems you are going through.

You are My child and know for sure,
My love for you is tender and pure.

Some things in life you simply must face,
But rest in My abundant grace.

No matter what your problem may be,
I want you to know it is important to Me.

Do not leave me out, please let me in,
I am your Lord and I am your friend.

All your concerns, I want to hear,
Your every problem, your every fear,

Because you are special and you must believe,
That you are very important to Me."

****

Promises for Worry

Behold, I am the Lord, the God of all flesh: is there any thing too hard for me?

Jeremiah 32:27

For the Lord is a sun and shield: the Lord will give grace and glory: no good thing will He withhold from them that walk uprightly.

Psalm 84:11

And he said, The things which are impossible with men are possible with God.

Luke 18:27

Eye hath not seen, nor ear heard, neither have entered into the heart of man, the things which God hath prepared for them that love him.

I Corinthians 2:9

It is of the Lord's mercies that we are not consumed, because his compassion fail not. They are new every morning: great is thy faithfulness.

Lamentations 3:23

97

Be careful for nothing; but in every thing by prayer and supplication with thanksgiving let your requests be made known unto God. And the peace of God, which passeth all understanding, shall keep your hearts and minds through Christ Jesus.

Philippians 4:6-7

Worry weighs a person down; an encouraging word cheers a person up.

Proverbs 12:25 (NLT)

Cast thy burden upon the LORD, and he shall sustain thee: he shall never suffer the righteous to be moved.

Psalm 55:22

Trust in the LORD with all thine heart; and lean not unto thine own understanding. In all thy ways acknowledge him, and he shall direct thy paths.

Proverbs 3:5-6

For I know the plans I have for you," declares the LORD, "plans to prosper you and not to harm you, plans to give you hope and a future.

Jeremiah 29:11 (NIV)

I want you to know, I want you to see,
That you are very important to Me.

Live Your Life

~

You

You

For it is God who works in you.
Philippians 2:13 (NIV)

Who are you?

What is your story?

What problems do you face?

How is God working in your life?

You may be facing a difficult situation today where you need God to work in your life. This book has given you the opportunity to look into the lives of some of the people in the Bible and see how God worked in their lives. The story, however, is not over. God also wants to work in your life. He is ready, willing, and able to help you in whatever difficult situation you may be facing today.

Despite what you may be going through, God can give you success in your troubles when you trust Him and give Him your life. Live your life according to the plan and purpose that He has for you. When you do, He will bless you and make you a blessing. Then your life will be a story that you can share with others. Just like the people you have read about in this book, you will have a story to tell.

You Can Show Us...

God can use you to bless others.
Whether through your life, testimonies, gifts, or service, you can be a blessing to others. As you walk with the Lord, you will be a godly example for others who are following in your footsteps.

God will give you gifts and talents.
God has given you gifts and talents that are uniquely and genuinely yours. You can use them to bless the Kingdom of God in a way in which no one else can.

God will give you a testimony.
Everyone will have difficulties and challenges in life. Although each person's experiences are unique, your testimony can be a source of inspiration and encouragement to those who are facing the storms of life.

May the LORD show you his favor
and give you his peace. Numbers 6:26 (NLT)

In Your Life…

How has your life blessed others?
Live so that your life can be a blessing to the Kingdom of God. Someone else can be uplifted, inspired, or encouraged by your work, and God can be glorified in your life.

How are you using your gifts and talents for God?
Find a way to use the gifts and talents that God has given you. Perhaps you can use them in your family, church, school, local community, or your job. As you pray and ask God for direction, He will show you what you can do.

How has God worked in your life?
Do you see how God is working in your life in the storms that you have endured? You can Share your testimony and inspire other people to trust God in their difficult times. Do not forget to share your story.

**Live so God can receive the glory,
Live and tell others your story.**

Your Story

Let the redeemed of the LORD tell their story—
those he redeemed from the hand of the foe,
Psalm 107:2 (NIV)

The Word of God is faithful and true,
A book that was written just for you.
But the Bible is not where the story ends.
For in every life, God will begin,
To reveal himself and show you,
How He can work in your life too.

Hear His voice and heed His call,
And give to Him your all and all,
And live so God can receive the glory,
Yes, live so you can share your story.

Write your story down on pages,
That others can read through the ages,
And see the things that you went through,
And how God worked them out for you.

****

Promises for You

Tell your children about it in the years to come, and let your children tell their children. Pass the story down from generation to generation.

Joel 1:3 (NLT)

Everyone will share the story of your wonderful goodness; they will sing with joy about your righteousness.

Psalm 145:7 (NLT)

This shall be written for the generation to come: and the people which shall be created shall praise the LORD.

Psalm 102:18

One generation shall praise thy works to another, and shall declare thy mighty acts.

Psalm 145:4

Let me proclaim your power to this new generation, your mighty miracles to all who come after me.

Psalm 71:18 (NLT)

Don't you realize that in a race everyone runs, but only one person gets the prize? So run to win!

1 Corinthians 9:24 (NLT)

But this one thing I do, forgetting those things which are behind, and reaching forth unto those things which are before, I press toward the mark for the prize of the high calling of God in Christ Jesus.

Philippians 3:13-14

But seek ye first the kingdom of God, and his righteousness; and all these things shall be added unto you.

Matthew 6:33

Look, I am coming soon! My reward is with me, and I will give to each person according to what they have done. I am the Alpha and the Omega, the First and the Last, the Beginning and the End.

Revelation 22:12-13 (NIV)

As long as it is day, we must do the works of him who sent me. Night is coming, when no one can work.

John 9:4 (NIV)

Write your story down on pages,
That others can read through the ages.

The Great Peace Series
for Christian Living

Finding Great Peace in the Word of God

The books in the *Great Peace Series for Christian Living* venture into the pages of the Bible and explore the lives of people just like you. In these books, you will learn how people with real problems experienced God in a real way during the difficult times of life. Each book includes biblical insights and inspirational poetry, as well as many pages of promises from the Word of God. Together, the Bible people, poetry, and promises will help you find the great peace that only God can give.

The Great Peace Series for Christian Living includes books for enduring the storms of life, beginning again, and facing each new day. The series also includes books written specifically for women, men, mothers, fathers, wives, husbands, parents, ministers, leaders, and more. Each book in the series has a companion journal that you can use to capture your personal thoughts and notes. Discover how you can find great peace in the Word of God through this series of inspirational books at www.GreatPeace.com.

ABOUT SHIRLEY D. HICKS

Shirley D. Hicks is a writer of Christian inspirational books and poetry. Her books in the *Great Peace Series for Christian Living* are a source of encouragement for people who are facing difficult and challenging times. After spending several years reading and studying the Bible, Shirley decided to pursue her passion for writing Christian books. Her writings have inspired and blessed many people. With Bachelor of Science degrees in Computer Science and Math, Shirley spent more than fifteen years as an IT professional. She also has a Master of Art degree in Theological Studies from Liberty University, Lynchburg, Virginia. She and her husband have one daughter. Visit her website at www.GreatPeace.com.

*Get the companion **Journal** to this book!*

The Great Peace for the Storms of Life Journal includes encouraging excerpts from the *Great Peace for the Storms of Life* book, plus one hundred pages for your journal entries. Get a copy today and write your story!

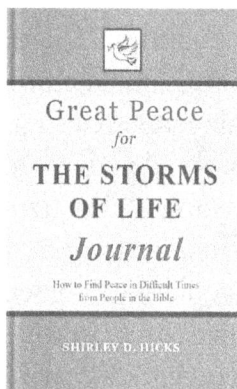

Great Peace
for
THE STORMS
OF LIFE
Journal

How to Find Peace in Difficult Times
from People in the Bible

SHIRLEY D. HICKS

The Great Peace for the Storms of Life JOURNAL

Available at
www.GreatPeace.com

After the storm is over…

Are you ready for a new beginning?

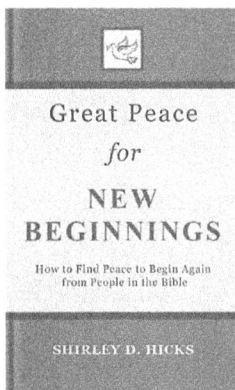

See all of the books in the

Great Peace Series for Christian Living

at

www.GreatPeace.com

www.ingramcontent.com/pod-product-compliance
Lightning Source LLC
Chambersburg PA
CBHW051043030426
42339CB00006B/170